CW00922621

About the Author

With almost four decades of her life spent as a soft skills trainer, Lesley Gibbons has run over 2,500 courses, for more than 15,000 delegates across six countries and two continents. Her clients have ranged from healthcare, nuclear power, house builders, civil servants and even a factory packaging food for prisoners. Flipcharts & Faux Pas is a compilation of a few of her most memorable recollections. Some are hilariously funny, some are quite sad and all of them are surprisingly real. A must read for soft skills trainers who have often asked themselves “is it just me?”

Flipcharts & Faux Pas

Hope you enjoy it!

Wes x

Lesley Gibbons

Flipcharts & Faux Pas

Olympia Publishers
London

www.olympiapublishers.com
OLYMPIA PAPERBACK EDITION

A CIP catalogue record for this title is
available from the British Library.

ISBN: 978-1-80074-867-5

This is a work of creative nonfiction. The events are portrayed to the
best of the author's memory. While all the stories in this book are true,
some names and identifying details have been changed to protect the
privacy of the people involved.

First Published in 2022

Olympia Publishers
Tallis House
2 Tallis Street
London
EC4Y 0AB

Printed in Great Britain

Dedication

I’ve so enjoyed writing this book and dedicate it to my Grandson Jack; the best retirement present I could have wished for.

## Acknowledgements

Few people actually knew that I was writing this book. Largely because I wanted to prove to myself that I could do it, and of course if I didn't get through to the print stage, then nobody would even know that I had tried. So, here I am with my first book deemed good enough to go to print, I'm now wanting to thank the very special people who contributed to my creation. 'The Starlets' were a powerful force back in the '80s and encouraged me to make that early jump from a Section Manager in Life Accounts to a fully-fledged member of the Training Department. Strange really, as I knew that Isla missed me carrying the rolled-up flipchart pad on the trains between the South-West, Leeds and London, Jod missed having a partner in crime to drive to Maidstone and back with in his beautifully polished blue Ford Mondeo and I certainly missed AJ's wit, giggling and sarcasm. On entering the scary and unknown world of freelancing, I was graced with so much support and advice it was truly overwhelming. Sharon was so helpful, and so professional, until the time when she introduced herself as Jack Daniels at a Training Associate dinner. I think her choice of drink that night had something to do with her forgetting her own name. Seriously though, Sharon has been amazing, and continues to be up there in the top portion of my friends list. I have to mention a few people who really helped me get my head around a VIP client with a challenging agenda. Shân, Jon, Ben and Nicola; you know what you did, so thank you. To Steve – thank you for all the opportunities to work with those very deserving staff in the healthcare industry. We had some laughs, a fair few challenges and many, many happy delegates. To Deborah and Frances – thank you for supporting me in that relationship, and offering much needed guidance and insight. PS Can we go for another afternoon tea soon? To all the training schedulers and administrators across the world – you do an amazing job of tying up trainers with dates, venues, delegates, printers and course materials. Thank you. And finally, to my wonderful and much-loved family who kept the wheels turning when I was working away from home, and knew exactly what to say when I'd experienced the 'group from hell'.

Chapter one

How it all started…

It was October 1981 and a skinny girl called Lesley was starting her first day in the new job. Well, perhaps even her first job as the months since leaving school in June had been filled 'contributing' to the '80s YTS at a local estate agent. A Youth Training Scheme that paid out £26 of Government money every week in return for a fantastic introduction to the world or work… tea making, typing onto a laminate and filling envelopes. No PCs, printers and definitely no emails in those days.

Lesley enjoyed the YTS and even more so, the banter with the staff in the office. Drinks after work and a lunchtime trip to Chelsea Girl became a regular event.

Not far from the estate agents was the tallest tower block in town. Apparently you could see the local and very famous racecourse from the top floor, and this fact alone was enough to make Lesley apply for a position as a Terminal Operator in the insurance company. Having been interviewed, (more of a chat really) for a generic position, she was offered a role where she knew nothing more than her job title.

So, that October Lesley found herself sitting at a desk on the sixth floor of the Life Accounts department. LIFE ACCOUNTS! How had this happened?

At no point did she say she was good at maths or enjoyed working with figures. She just wanted to sit on a chair and type. After all Lesley had successfully passed her typing exams that summer and let's just say that her typing grade was significantly higher than her maths grade. Just to make this first day even worse, Lesley learnt that the top floor was the restaurant, and nobody had a desk up there.

'Oh well,' I thought, 'everyone seems very friendly.' And before I knew it, I was paying my deposit for the much talked about Christmas 'do'. Tradition dictated that the office emptied at midday and headed down to the local hotel for a sophisticated three course meal and the predictable disco till early evening. Spilling out onto the pavement and into the nearest pub was a must and getting home before midnight was unheard of. I must add at this point that it was a midweek event and unless we were one of the few who got to the boss first to book a day's leave, we had to turn up for work as usual the next day.

So, was it at this point, when I was caring for my drunk, sad or emotional colleagues, that I realised I wanted a career where I could help others? Surely not!

A career where I could encourage others to reflect on their behaviour and I could promote discussion and reflection by asking some very relevant questions. Some of these memories are pretty vague, mind you, and the only question I probably asked on that first Christmas initiation was 'Do you really need another White Lightening, or do you think you'll be sick again?'

Winding forward by three years and I'm now a Section Manager. Still in Life Accounts with a fantastic team supporting me and with some great friends; many of whom I still see today. Strangely enough we try and get together every March for a race day of drinking, eating, betting on the horses and of course catching up. Not surprisingly this happens at that racecourse that you can apparently get a good view of from the top floor.

Since the Covid-19 pandemic, I've really missed not being able to see 'The Starlets'; Isla, Jod, Vize, Clara, Shazza, AJ, Mincer, Wiffers, Lex, and Spanner. I'm thinking, and hoping, that the next meetup will be a really good one!

So, what did a Section Manager actually do in this Insurance Company? Well, as there were two of us with our own teams (picked by the 'scores on the doors, names in the frames' reference to the game show The Generation Game), I was fortunate to be able to focus on the 'soft skills' development of the people. My colleague, the other Section Manager who I will call Isla (after Isla St Clair from that very game show), focused on the technical development of the people. We made a great team; despite the fact that Isla started to call me Deirdre, after the lady with large glasses and curly hair off Coronation Street. In fact, he still calls me that now!

Time rolled on and one of the Senior Managers told me about a vacancy in the Training department. The team was based in a different building and I was reluctant to leave my colleagues and friends behind, however after a more thorough interview and a mini presentation this time, I got the job. I was now a Training Consultant in an environment where everybody talked about growth, development, objectives, training courses and OHP slides. I knew that my experience of typing onto laminate in 1981 would help my

career in the end.
So, armed with a brown tan briefcase, and always with a spare OHP bulb and a few flipchart pens, I became the roving trainer I'd wanted to be.

This book shares my most memorable experiences between then and March 2020 when I retired. In that month Covid-19 wiped my diary as all events were cancelled, people were working from home or furloughed and travel very much restricted, so I made the tough yet best decision to quit whilst it was good. I had the most amazing thirty-nine years doing what I loved; travelling across the UK, Europe and Middle East, and now have the luxury of time to sit down and write about the moments that will stay with me forever.

For those reading this who were or are a soft skills trainer, I bet you can relate to many of my personal experiences. It's a tiring and often challenging job, yet oh so rewarding. I certainly made the most of '*that career where I could encourage others to reflect on their behaviour and I could promote discussion and reflection by asking some very relevant questions.*'

Here's how those thirty-nine years looked…

1981 Insurance
1997 Banking
2006 Self-employed freelancer
2015 Director of a Limited Company – still a freelancer
2020 Retired, happy and loving spending time with my family, including my baby Grandson.

Chapter two

Introductions from Delegates

I love this early part of delivering a training course. Not only is it an opportunity to gain an insight into why these people are attending, it's a chance to sense how they may be feeling about it.

Body language and tone of voice speaks volumes and often gave me a sense of something deeper than their words alone. The nervous delegate, the one who struggles to speak out loud in a group setting, the one who thinks they know it all…

With a large group the introductions can sound a little repetitive and take up more valuable time than you'd hoped. You know that you need to be at a certain point in the course by coffee break (often because your 'trainer script' tells you so), and at the rate this is going you'll be lucky to get there by lunchtime! This is why I never ever shared the timetable with my groups; only the content we would be covering.

Naturally in this introductory session I would make a handwritten note of the important stuff they shared like their personal objectives and specific things they were hoping to have covered on the course. I would always keep these notes on the table in case we needed to refer back to them. Occasionally however, an introduction would throw me a surprise and I would choose to capture it in my personal notes later in the day… for when I was writing my book.

These introductions still make me laugh now, and isn't it strange that I can remember who that person was, where they worked and even what they were wearing.

<u>Haircut</u>

"I need to break for lunch at 11.50 a.m. I've booked a haircut and won't be back till around two p.m." Interestingly, when that person returned from lunch their hair looked no different.

<u>Buttons</u>

"Can nobody in this room fiddle with any buttons please. I have a phobia of buttons… In fact, I can't talk about it any more."

<u>Dog</u>

"I need to bring my dog into the course with me tomorrow. We have a vet's appointment straight after and I won't have time to go home and get him."

<u>Mad dash</u>

"Please don't move me around the room today, I need to stay by the door as I have an upset stomach."

<u>Really?</u>

"This is my second week in the company and I hate it. Everyone is so up themselves; especially the managers." (This was on an in-house management training course where all the delegates worked for this same company.)

Chapter three

Interesting journeys

As you can imagine over thirty-nine years, I've used almost every mode of transport to get to and from a training venue. Planes, trains, automobiles, tube, tram, bus and even a mini-bus alongside the desert in the searing heat; more of that later. Some venues were in city centres, some in the middle of nowhere, some rough and some very posh.

In most cases, the travelling was part of the enjoyment and I would set off with my trainers notes and flipchart pens and use the journey as time to prepare for the course I was about to deliver. In most cases this worked well and meant that I was ready to set up the room and relax before the delegates arrived. In some cases however, my journey was a distraction and my planned preparation hadn't been as thorough as I had hoped.

Home to London by train

Pre-booked tickets with a seat reservation usually meant that I was sitting in the same seat on every journey. This was often the case for my fellow travellers too. Monday morning meant lady with dark green suit that reminded me of my school uniform. Wednesday morning was a young chap who boarded the train looking like he'd spent the weekend in a bus shelter, and arrived in London in a pristine black suit; bus shelter clothing now safely scrunched into a Tesco bag for life.

A lady (I use that term loosely), used to join the train one stop after mine. Well dressed and very well spoken. She'd drink her coffee then put her flask away and get out a small pink purse, a box of man size tissues and a white carrier bag. The remaining one hour and fifty-five minutes of her journey was spent cleaning out her nails with the metal nail file from the pink purse, collecting the dirt in a tissue and putting the tissues into the white carrier bag. Believe me, on some mornings that carrier bag was full by the time we arrived in London. I was half tempted to buy her a nail brush and a bar of soap to use before she boarded the train but in the end I did the sensible thing and started booking a seat in the quiet carriage, knowing that I'd be away from the sight of her morning ritual. Those small metal nail files with the curved end still take me back to that time.

Birmingham to Glasgow by plane

During my banking days I used to travel to some of the large administration centres across the UK. Sometimes for a TNA (Training Needs Analysis), and sometimes to deliver a programme. Glasgow was home to one of our largest sites and a flight up with a colleague to spend a few days in the office was now becoming an urgent need. Our affiliated travel booking service purchased the necessary tickets and before we knew it Jo and I were about to board a Flybe plane to Glasgow. Our seats were right at the back of the plane and as we walked down the aisle we were asked to wait a moment. One of the cabin crew had her hand over her nose and was spraying profusely around our seats and inside the toilet.

This went on for some time and the smell reaching us half-way down the plane was nauseating. A mixture of cheap air freshener and something I'd rather not think about. Finally we were encouraged to make our way to our seats and received an immediate apology. Apparently a passenger on the inbound flight had suffered an upset stomach and made full use of the facilities. All seemed well and we took off without delay, however the one smell; not the air freshener, the other one, started to return. It stayed with us for the remainder of the flight and, indeed, through the passenger terminal on arrival at Glasgow. In the taxi to our hotel, Jo and I sensed that the smell was following us. At the hotel we checked in and handed over our credit cards as security for the hotel in case we decided to empty the mini bar and steal all the towels. You know when someone stands at a hotel reception and they need to get into their bag so they put the bag up on the counter… well, this is what Jo did. A look of horror and disgust passed across her face as she looked at me and pointed to the mess her bag had left on the reception counter. Yep, you've guessed it; it was the earlier mentioned result of the passengers upset stomach who had obviously left a very runny deposit on the floor of the plane by Jo's seat.

There's always a bonus when travelling to a destination and arriving before the end of the working day. The shops are still open and in Jo's case, a much needed new handbag was only a short walk away.

Aberdeen to Birmingham by plane

This was a regular trip for me; I'd fly up one day, stay the night then fly back after my course had ended the following day. I didn't mind this trip at all as the shopping centre in Aberdeen was always worth a look and the food court had some of my most loved restaurants. One November the fog had been hanging around all day and I was amazed that my flight out of Birmingham had even gone ahead. My flight out of Aberdeen the following evening however was a different story. The fog was dense and rolling in off the sea and with only a few minutes before my flight was due to depart, the announcement came that all flights out of Aberdeen were now cancelled. I didn't have any work planned for the following day so a night in a Premier Inn and a coach to take me and the other passengers back to the airport the following morning didn't seem too daunting. The coach journey the following morning however was a strong indication that still no flights would be leaving as the fog was worse than the previous evening. True enough, at check-in it was confirmed that the flight was cancelled and a coach had been arranged to drive us down to Birmingham Airport that day. Breakfast vouchers were handed out and an egg muffin was quickly consumed before boarding the coach. Thankfully there was a toilet onboard, and the driver seemed friendly enough – well, he was smiling which was good as I could understand little of what he was actually saying in his very broad Scottish accent. One thing I did notice; he said 'Ken' after many of his sentences. Surely he didn't think I was a male called Ken did he?

Moving forward by ten hours and fifteen minutes to be

precise, the coach finally arrives at Birmingham Airport. My car park ticket expired just over twenty-six hours ago so £84 later I finally joined the M42 and headed for home.

London to Basel by plane

I was really excited about this trip. Not only was it a second chance to deliver training in Switzerland which I'd loved the first time, it was to deliver a course I'd written (always a pleasure). My flight took me from London Heathrow to Basel-Mulhouse-Freiburg and was pretty standard with the usual excellent service from KLM. I wish I had done my research before I arrived though, as I'd have known that the airport served three countries and was located across the borders of Switzerland, France and Germany. Passport control and luggage collection was smooth and before long I was walking down a corridor where I would expect to see a driver at the end holding a board with my name on. After some time looking I realised that I'd been stood up and when I enquired at the information desk I was spoken to in French. In front of me was a map of Mulhouse and I was expecting to see one of Basel. I'd clearly ended up in France instead of Switzerland so using my very dodgy French speaking skills I explained that I needed to be in Basel. I was quickly escorted through a number of doors and corridors back to the baggage collection area and through a different door and corridor where my driver was waiting for me. Indeed, he was the only driver waiting in arrivals so I guess all the other passengers had done their research and taken the correct door in the first place. I'm just thankful I hadn't taken the door into Germany as my linguist ability on this subject is nil!

This journey was snow joke

One of my most memorable venues to run a course in was a very old hotel in the South West. About a forty-minute drive from home and steeped in history, it reminded me of Upstairs Downstairs, or Downton Abbey in today's world. My training room was the library where delegates would sit on large sofas in front of a log fire. Tea and coffee with homemade shortbread was brought in every few hours and when the weather was good we could take a walk in our lunch break around the gardens of this beautiful hotel.

On the final day of a January course, the log fire was a much-needed asset and a walk around the garden was out of the question. By four p.m. when we had finished the course the sky was white and a few snowflakes were starting to fall. My journey home was up and over a hill so I knew that I needed to leave soon before the snow became a concern. Twenty minutes into my journey and I was approaching the hill. All looked fine yet the sky was still white. Then everything changed. A blizzard of huge snowflakes started to fall and within five minutes we were at a standstill on this busy A-road. Five hours later and nobody had moved. People were taking a pee outside their cars and engines were now quiet. Feeling slightly vulnerable, tired, hungry and cold (and no I hadn't carried the recommended blanket, phone charger and food just in case), I saw an older couple shuffle towards my car. They'd been parked next to me all this time and noticed I was on my own so invited me to their car to charge my phone and devour a packet of crisps until things started moving. They had to kick the snow away so I could open my car door to get out.

We chatted in their car until about eleven p.m. when things started to move and cars in front were edging along slowly towards a roundabout. Vehicles were now moving on the opposite carriageway so it was obvious that drivers weren't driving over the roundabout and down the hill but driving around it and back on themselves. I thanked the elderly couple and wished them a safe journey home. They'd just flown into Heathrow from India and must've been feeling worse than I did, yet they were so kind. Two hours and ten minutes later I finally arrived home. The motorway had been completely free from snow and whilst it had added over fifty miles to my journey, I was home and that's all that mattered.

Ten a.m. the following morning and I got a call from the elderly couple who had been so kind. They wanted to check I was okay. Whilst I'd arrived home at 1.10 a.m., they were still travelling at 4.30 a.m. so I'd definitely made the right decision to turn around and take another route. I will definitely remember that journey, however rather than fuelling my memory with how bad it was, I remember the two people who made it so much better. In 2021 there's a well-known phrase and they certainly lived up to it.

'Be Kind.'

Chapter four

Best and Worst Hotels

As most roving trainers will be familiar, I've stayed in literally hundreds of hotels throughout my career. It's fair to say that they've ranged from the most awful and basic to the most luxurious with frills and mod cons. For all my foreign trips the client had booked the hotel for me, and thankfully they were definitely in the 'best hotel' category. From five-star luxury in the Crowne Plaza in Kuwait with its nine restaurants and incredible outdoor pool, to the beautiful suite overlooking Lake Geneva… made even better with its great view of the Jet d'Eau. I've been truly spoilt.

Closer to home, The Rocks in Dunbar was a real treat. A bathtub overlooking the sea, a plush and well-equipped room and a gorgeous Scottish breakfast in the morning. I fully recommend the scrambled egg and smoked salmon. Back into England in Suffolk, and the Westleton Crown is an example of how to get it right. Small yet beautifully decorated rooms filled with treats to eat and toiletries to pamper with on a stunning coastline. William and Kate stayed there once for a friend's wedding, so if it's good enough for them… you know the rest.

It would be unkind and probably a bit foolish to name the worst hotels I've experienced and to be fair, there haven't been that many. Some would be in the worst category because of their location rather than the hotel itself.

Checking into a hotel for the first time I found exciting; not knowing what my room will be like and what's on the breakfast menu for the morning. It's certainly true that you have a 'moment of truth' as you walk into a hotel lobby and you know whether it's already matching your expectations. Websites can be so misleading and I'm convinced that some of the photos I saw were, indeed, artist impressions, as the real thing bared no resemblance whatsoever.

Working on an all-inclusive rate meant that I could choose how much of my daily rate to spend on travel and accommodation. Obviously if I went for a five-star hotel every time I wouldn't have much left after I had deducted all my expenses. The same goes for travel. A return coach trip to London would cost as little as £11.75 a day compared to a first class return train ticket at over £300. So, occasionally when hotels were few and far between, I did have to go with one that I could just about tolerate for a night or two, and in these instances, I made sure I carried my 'rescue pack'. For any current trainers reading this, maybe my list is a must in your suitcase or laptop bag.

- A small, see-through plastic bag for a remote control. Imagine all the grubby hands transmitting bacteria to their favourite channel buttons.

- A mug and spoon with some tea bags or coffee sachets. I even made sure I rinsed the kettle out three times before using it. A silicone collapsible mug was invaluable.

- Slippers or socks. Even if the carpets or bathroom tiles looked like they had been vacuumed.

Thankfully, one of my earliest memories of staying in a hotel for work is a good one and I only have to look at a bottle of Baileys to reignite those recollections.

The Empress Hotel in Douglas, Isle of Man became almost a second home back in the late '80s. I would fly out of Birmingham Airport with Manx Airlines on a Monday morning and fly back home often on the Wednesday or Thursday. The flight into the Isle of Man always ended with a three-legged chocolate as you left the aircraft, and the taxi driver taking me to my hotel would be obliging enough to point out the fairy bridge as we drove down the valley towards Douglas. Apparently if you said hello to the fairies out loud you would have a good stay on the island. I'm not sure if that was true as apart from falling over in an underground car park and cutting my leg open once, my trips were a success.

So, back to The Empress Hotel. I used to meet my work friend there as she moved out to live on the island and we would sit in the Piano Bar and enjoy a Baileys on ice whilst looking out to sea and catching up. It's a shame really as the office we worked from no longer exists, Manx Airlines went bust and those three-legged chocolates are a distant memory. I hope the fairies are still there and not missing me too much.

Chapter five

Poorly Delegates

We've all been there I'm sure… we wake up in the morning feeling unwell and probably not fit for work. As a trainer with a planned course to deliver and a group of delegates who have planned their workload around this event, you get out of bed, take the necessary medication and get on with it. Ok, you may be not delivering that course in your usual style of all four cylinders firing, but you get through it.

I'm fortunate to say that I've only had to cancel or postpone on four occasions; all for what I believe were credible reasons. (Hospital admission, longer than planned recovery from surgery, vomiting and fainting.) Not even a broken foot kept me away from one group although I did deliver that course sitting down with my black, platformed and highly fashionable NHS boot on.

I've often wondered if some delegates make the usual sacrifices and turn up for a course when they should have really stayed at home. Equally, I've had delegates turn up who profess to be very unwell and somehow make a miraculous recovery once they're told that there's no roleplay or cringy activities built into the content.

Sadly, for some individuals concerned, they really were poorly and in my opinion made the wrong decision to turn up for training.

Poor Paul

Take Paul, a Senior Manager in the aerospace industry. He was sitting furthest away from me so I dread to think how bad the smell was for his nearest colleagues in the room. I was mid talking and using my perfectly drawn flipchart image to bring some theory to life, when he quickly stood up and walked very slowly towards the door. He was hunched over with his knees touching and his feet further apart. With a pained look on his face he left the training room, and behind him the most awful smell. Needing to know if he'd left anything on his chair, I walked over to his table where the remaining three delegates were now holding their noses, sniggering and looking around them with the same worries that I had. Poor Paul. He would have had to make his way down two flights of stairs, out the door onto a short walkway and in through another door to get to the gents. We will never know if he 'made it in time', as none of us were brave enough to ask when he returned nearly two hours later wearing a different pair of trousers and a sheepish grin. I think he was grateful that I hadn't asked any embarrassing questions, as he presented me with a glowing evaluation form and a little 'Thank you' written on the bottom at the end of the day.

Bandages

Somewhere in the West I was running a course for a large group of analysts. I loved working with them and over a few days generally got to know more about each of them and how they preferred to work. I would definitely say that the majority of the group were reflective and introvert so I spent quite a bit of time engaging with them in small groups or individually.

Being an apparent introvert myself, I'm more than flexible when it comes to delivering a course in a way that appeals to everyone, rather than assuming one style fits all. I know what it's like to be a delegate on a course where the trainer assumes that everyone is just like them.

One delegate was becoming noticeably uncomfortable throughout the first morning and started standing up and stretching during small group discussions. After what was probably the third time of me noticing, I asked this person to join me for a quick chat outside the training room. In a roundabout way I asked if there was anything I needed to know or do to make them more comfortable. As soon as I'd started talking, they crossed their arms over their chest and shook their head, disengaged the eye contact and told me they were okay. Fine I thought… I can only ask. Later that day, during a coffee break, one of the venue administrators came to tell me that the delegate had fainted and they'd called an ambulance. I wasn't to expect them back that afternoon and could I pop into the office after I'd ended the course that day. In the office I was told that this poor person had recently started their transgender journey and their chest bandages had been wrapped too tight causing the problem. This story left me sad for ages, however I did see that person again in another venue, and they were smiling, which made me smile too.

Meatball mistake

Delivering a course in a town or city centre venue usually meant a longer break at lunchtime as many delegates want to make use of the shopping and food opportunities.

I too used to love an opportunity to take a walk and a browse in the fresh air during my lunch break and still have enough time to get back into the training room and prepare for the afternoon.

Some take-away food outlets offered weekday specials and one day it became known that the Wednesday special just down the road was a hot meatball baguette. Not my kind of thing at all, however some of my group were excited to get there early and make their purchase before the meatballs ran out. Mid-afternoon it soon became apparent that more than half of the group had made the same choice. The hot meatball baguettes were reappearing in liquid form. The course was abandoned for the day and my evening challenge was to now work out how to fit into an already busy second day the content that we'd missed. Needless to say, two of the poorly delegates didn't make it back for day two. I remained smug and thankful for my cheese pasta salad choice and vowed never to eat from this take-away food outlet.

Co-trainer faux pas

I truly believe that you need to have a connection with the trainer that you're co-delivering an event. It needs to be a slick and seamless process to switch from one person to the other with no unprofessional contradictions or digs. It's most definitely not a competition to become the most popular trainer out of the pair.

Co-delivering certainly gets easier as you get to know the other trainer and you come away from an event having learnt something about how they delivered their sessions.

It's a valuable opportunity to reflect on your own style and ask yourself how you would've answered that question or responded to that comment.

Imagine the other trainer is someone you know really well. You ate together the previous evening and you travelled to the venue in the same car. They even tell you that last night's dinner is causing a rumbling in their stomach that cannot be ignored. With only twenty minutes before the course is due to start, Jane releases an almighty amount of wind and quickly admits that a toilet visit is needed. Positioned with one hand over my nose and the other clutching a particularly expensive body spray, I start squirting into the air just as our first delegate arrives. It's obvious that he's walked into an embarrassing situation, and probably thinks that it was me who made the offending smell. What can you do but walk back to your bag and put the expensive body spray away and say nothing. Jane returns after what I can only hope was a productive toilet visit and the course starts as planned.

The morale of this story is that whatever your co-trainer has done you never drop them in it. You remain professional, stick to the plan, and carry on. It wasn't until the journey back home in the car that Jane found out what had happened and I made a mental note to restock on body spray if we were ever co-delivering again.

Chapter six

Offensive or just Funny?

I am perfectly aware that as a soft skills trainer there is usually an expectation that I will talk a lot; and that's certainly the case when I'm delivering a theory session. Of course, there has to be a necessary balance of listening too and an opportunity to show to your delegates that you really care about what they say. Being a reflective person myself, my friends and family are used to me listening to what they have to say and feeling comfortable if I don't speak for a while. I don't always feel the need to fill silence with words.

I think being a trainer is such a transparent role and I know that many delegates like to second guess what I'm thinking. I know this because a few have told me over the years. Just as I do with them, they observe my body language and notice subtle changes in my tone of voice. So, what do you do when you're faced with a person or a situation that leaves you speechless. Literally speechless.

A young, all male group of delegates were the epitome of cheekiness from the start of the day. They had lots to say; not always relevant to the course, and little patience for listening. It can take a while to bond with this kind of group but perseverance and cheekiness on my part gets us to somewhere close. (I think that's mirroring and matching isn't it?) We'd had a productive morning and with some tweaking to the course style and content, we had managed to break for lunch on time.

Well, what busy bees those chaps had been during their lunch break. My trip to the local sandwich deli had given them the perfect opportunity to stay in the training room and get creative.

Of course, I knew nothing of their lunch break mischief when I started the afternoon session, however as I turned over for a clean piece of flipchart paper I saw the fruits of their labour. A cartoon drawing of something very rude, and the next page, another well-drawn yet very rude image. I was speechless, they were in fits of laughter and I was probably very red in the face. Thankfully, the fourth page was clear and ready for me to use. How do you go on to draw up your image on Tuckman's Team Evolution after that?

I remember observing some unusual behaviours when working with delegates from a particular organisation in the West, and to begin with I was intrigued. Over the years these behaviours almost went unnoticed as I got used to the organisation and the talent it recruited. Body jolt tics were something I would see maybe half a dozen times in a year, and verbal tics would occasionally present themselves in the training room. So, how do you cope with a verbal tic which is actually a burp? This person would end every single sentence, and sometimes a comma pause too, with a burp. Of course, professional to the last, I wouldn't dream of commenting, yet I'm sure my facial expressions gave it away. Disbelief (did I just hear that right?), turns to disgust, turns to a real need to laugh out loud. I'm left wondering what that sort of damage that constant burping does to their digestive system. I'm glad to say that I will never know.

Purpose-built or designed training venues are just great. They have all the facilities you need to make your course a memorable and productive one. A photocopier, a well-stocked stationery cupboard, a fridge and a microwave. I've seen some strange concoctions brought into to the course in Tupperware boxes ready to microwave at lunchtime. Roast potatoes and sprouts, curry and rice (should you ever reheat cooked rice?), even steak and chips. I'm always more than happy for delegates to get their lunch and bring it back into the training room to eat it. Some would use this opportunity to read back through the notes they'd made in the morning, or check the latest news updates on their phones. And yes, unfortunately some of those microwave blasted lunches have been a little potent on the nostrils. If there's one dish you should never consume in a confined space like a training room… it's a fish pie. The smell is with you all afternoon. It's in my nostrils, it's attacking my coat, and even worse, it's still there the next day. That's not at all funny; it's offensive!

Maybe this memory is the funniest and most offensive of all. Again with a delegate somewhere in the West, he arrives in a Roger the Dodger knitted jumper. Fair play if this was hand-knitted as it was brilliant and certainly created some discussion before we got started on the introductions. Roger the Dodger filled most of the front of this jumper so his features were clear to see. Characteristic black spiky hair, chubby cheeks and a red and black check jumper.

The delegate wearing Roger, let's call him James, clearly

loves his jumper. In fact, James thinks he's helping Roger by placing his forefinger on Roger's nose, moving it around, then placing said finger in his own mouth. This went on for all of the day. James was picking Roger's woolly nose and eating it! Offensive and funny? Most definitely both I think. Poor Roger. Has he never heard of a decongestant?

Chapter seven

Polishing our Presentation Skills

Delivering a Presentation Skills course was definitely in my top three of most enjoyable events to run. I loved the visible changes it brought to those very nervous delegates who, at the beginning didn't think they had the confidence to stand up and talk, to becoming someone who walked away feeling relieved, confident and most of all proud of what they'd achieved.

It's fair to say that I've trained delegates from both ends of the spectrum. Those who were so nervous they managed to vomit over the desk or floor (and probably a few in the toilet that never even told me!), to those who were so confident they couldn't wait to get started. I found it fascinating that a few of those 'cocky, confident' types did such a bad job and fell apart when they stood up to talk. Equally some of those very nervous presenters managed to pull a rabbit out of a hat and deliver the most polished and compelling presentations I've ever seen.

Occasionally the group got allocated a topic to write a presentation on. I loved these days as it was always an opportunity to brush up on a subject that was clearly very relevant to the delegates. The downside of course was that it became a little repetitive after you've heard half a dozen presentations on the same subject. When there was no topic given the groups would usually choose a hobby, a particular holiday destination or sporting achievement to talk about. I loved these as you never knew what you were going to be listening to.

I couldn't pull this book together without listing a few of the most interesting or surprising presentations I've listened to.

Chicken fillets – one theatre nurse wanted to present the benefits of paying for better quality gloves. She brought in three different pairs of gloves and two raw chicken fillets. Thankfully she did mention in her introduction that vegetarians could just listen if they preferred. Imagine the chicken fillets getting warmer as they were handed to each person and examined with three different pairs of gloves. The idea was to vote on the gloves that made the chicken fillets easier to handle, and it worked. The highest votes went to the most expensive pair of gloves. I thought it was great how this nurse turned her presentation into a survey and presented lots of data to support her quest. I usually love to get involved like the delegates do however on this occasion there was no way I could take a now very pale, sticky and probably smelly raw chicken fillet and make any sensible contribution. I could only hope that the nurse disposed of them in the right hospital bin and they weren't left unattended till the end of her shift.

Rubik's cube – now I could never solve the puzzle of the Rubik's cube. After getting one side all the same colour I used to give up out of frustration and boredom. So, imagine my surprise when one young delegate chose to deliver a ten-minute presentation on the cube. How would he fill all that time? Well, I needn't have worried as it was fascinating to hear about their history, the skill, the mental agility, the price and the shapes.

The shapes! I thought a cube was a cube. Not in this case as I learnt that you can get a Rubik's cube in the shape of a pyramid, a diamond, an almost circle, and even a snake. I was thoroughly hooked, not just by what I was hearing but what I was seeing too. This chap has been working the traditional square Rubik's cube throughout his presentation and in the tenth minute he had solved the puzzle. All six sides were perfect, we'd learnt loads about the cube and this chap had remained calm, maintained eye contact with his audience and spoke fluently throughout. I wonder how many in the group have since bought their own Rubik's cube? PS Not me! Maybe one day.

Deadly cheesy – some presentations fill you with happiness and hope, whilst others remind you of the sad and often upsetting situations we come across. One lady who worked in an admin area of a hospital decided to present on a cost saving idea she'd had. Sadly it was her job to liaise with the local council when a deceased persons family were unable to meet the costs of the funeral. Her presentation style was perfect as she showed empathy and understanding as well as a realistic business view… until she showed her first bullet point list on a slide. The bullet points weren't points at all; they were funeral cars.

Every time she revealed the next line on her list a funeral car would enter the slide from the right, zoom across to the left and reverse into spot before the associated words came into view. Now I'm all for making a presentation light-hearted and fun but really?

What's wrong with the traditional bullet point that quietly appears when you need it?

• Don't let your bullet points distract the audience from the main message.

• If there's a chance that someone could be offended, don't use it.

• Some subjects can be made as cheesy as you like, however some need to be left plain and simple.

Ginger biscuits – I was really looking forward to this one. A delegate was planning to deliver a presentation on ginger biscuits and wanted to emphasise that a good one needed to appeal to all four Learning Styles (Honey & Mumford). So there was a bit of talking, some interaction, some theory and detail and even a demonstration. Only once have I been given a training room with an oven in it, and sadly that wasn't on this occasion. So the delegate would have to weigh the ingredients and mix them up, then stop at the 'ready for oven' stage. Sounded great in theory eh? Reality was that ten minutes later the desk, the presenter and my keyboard were covered in white flour. The carpet was dotted with lumps of sticky, brown ginger biscuit mixture and the group have now had their appetites whetted and are in serious need of a tea break with real, edible biscuits.

I can't fault anyone for trying. I only wish I'd taken my vacuum cleaner and cleaning wipes on that day. Instead I left the resident cleaner an apology note and made a swift exit before she arrived.

Chapter eight

A Middle Eastern Delight

It's November 2006 and I'm just about getting enough work to convince myself that I've done the right thing in stepping out of the corporate world of being employed. I remind myself that it's only been six weeks since I started out on my own, yet I already feel more relaxed, more in control of my own goals and definitely free from the senior managers who like to take credit for work they were barely involved in. That's not a dig by the way, as I believe that those types of people exist in any large corporate business. It's sad but true. Perhaps most surprisingly, I was ready for my next challenge, and I hadn't felt like that in a very long time. Little did I know that my next challenge was about to show its face big time.

I received a call from an old colleague of mine asking if I would be prepared to deliver a course overseas. She had been flying out to Dubai fairly often to deliver training for a variety of job roles and cultures and an urgent need had been identified that had to be addressed in the next three days. So, two days later I'm on an Emirates flight to Dubai. I had to pick up my flight ticket from Birmingham airport, prepare for the course on the flight itself with some very sketchy materials that I'd had emailed to me, and meet the owner of the training company that afternoon in Downtown

Dubai. My hotel had been booked for me and a driver would be there to meet me when I land.

I'm not great with surprises and I do like to plan ahead, so this trip, at such short notice, was definitely pushing me out of my comfort zone. Instead of preparing for the course I was delivering, I was now spending the valuable six and a half hours flight time reading up about Middle Eastern culture, the area and generally panicking about everything that could go wrong. Oh, and I was also wondering if I should actually eat the airplane food I'd been given, because it was red, it smelt spicy and most worryingly of all, it could give me an upset stomach.

The first thing that struck me was the heat when I left the airport terminal in Dubai. I wasn't entirely sure if it was due to the number of people around me (seriously it was like being in the crowd at a Premiership Rugby game), or if it really was the temperature of the air. It took me around twenty minutes to spot my name on a clipboard and follow my driver out to the car. I was now known as Miss Lesley. I guess my first few hours in Dubai had gone well and without incident. After settling into my hotel room my next task was to find the office of the training company owner. I kind of expected a debrief on the company history, the range of courses they offer and hopefully a little about the delegates I would be training the next day. Well, that's what I was hoping for after my treacherous walk across dusty, broken pavements to find the well-concealed office. Instead, I had the briefest of introduction, the longest of interrogation about confidentiality and copyright and a brief parting of good luck with a brown envelope pushed into my hand.

I was asked to open the envelope before I left the office, and when I did I found £300 British pounds and a note listing the time I would be collected from my hotel in the morning, the venue of my course and the strict timings of the day, and the time I would be collected to be driven back to the airport for my flight home. I guessed I didn't need to invoice for this one then.

So, with the rest of the day to myself, I organised a driver with the hotel reception and went off to explore. First stop was the Burj Al Arab… not inside of course (that would happen some nine years later with my sister as a birthday treat), and then the Emirates shopping mall with its indoor ski slope. I shopped, not skied by the way. I didn't explore for long as I now had some much-needed course preparation to do and a good night's sleep was required to ensure I was in tip top trainer mode the next morning.

The worst bit about the training day itself was the journey to and from the venue which was a most beautiful hotel overlooking the beach. I was in the midst of five lanes of erratic drivers all using their mobile phones and drinking out of a paper cup. I was beginning to wish that I too had a paper cup… filled with gin to erase the feeling of sheer fright in the back of the executive car. The rest of the day was amazing. The service from the hotel was impeccable with petit fours and dried fruits and nuts brought in every half an hour, and bottles of ice-cold water and jugs of the strongest coffee I have ever had. The delegates held a variety of roles and originated from India, Australia and the UK and told fascinating stories about their lives in Dubai.

I'm not sure if I ever gave myself a real pat on the back during my career, however the feeling I had at the end of that course confirmed that I was doing what I loved and that I'd actually thrived on the challenges this trip had set me. Little did I know that this short trip to the Middle East had prepared me for a much longer and more challenging trip years later.

Four years later to be precise, only this time I wasn't alone. Sharon, my talented co-trainer who soon became, and still is, a true friend, was with me as we headed up into the skies bound for Kuwait. I was using a different airline this time, and a need to land in Bahrain and board another plane to Kuwait, so the journey was quite a bit longer. We had our first eye opening moment in Bahrain when we realised that we should have packed some scarves in our hand luggage to wrap around our chests. It seemed that our eyes weren't the only ones to be well and truly opened! With scarves purchased and appropriately worn we started to notice men who had bright orange powder in their beards. A little bit like those Tam O Shanter hats and orange beard sets you can hire in a fancy-dress shop. I was so relieved to be with Sharon as we soon became circled by these gentlemen and most definitely started to feel like the cabaret everyone had to see.

Fast forward a few hours and we're in our five-star Crowne Plaza hotel in Farwaniya, Kuwait. We were keen to get some essential preparation under our belt for our first day of delivery however the need to explore was greater.

We made a verbal agreement to try either the outdoor or indoor pool during our stay, and at least two of the nine restaurants. At check-in we had been given a pass that took us into a VIP lounge where complimentary snacks and drinks were available 24/7 so a quick bite to eat before that essential preparation was a welcome treat. In fact, it too was essential as we had to be up, showered and eaten all by 7.30 a.m. to be collected by our driver to take us to the training venue.

Remember in Dubai I had an executive car and driver taking me to and from the venue? Well, you can imagine my disappointment when a very old and noisy minibus arrived to make that important journey. It was bereft of air conditioning so the windows just had to be opened. Even at 7.30 a.m. the temperature was in the 30s and our long-sleeved tops (had to be long-sleeved) were now starting to feel uncomfortable. Within five minutes we were covered in the sand that was now blowing in through the open windows as we sped along the very busy roads. So, the choice was either to get swelteringly hot with the windows closed, or covered in sand and marginally cooler with the windows open. Anyone who knows me and my curly hair would have correctly guessed that we had no choice but to go for the hot and closed option.

Because of the intense heat in Kuwait, our training day ended at 1.30 p.m., and Sharon and I were handed some breakfast and lunch vouchers to use in their onsite restaurant.

We wondered how we could possibly fit in a breakfast break and a lunch break and still deliver the content we needed to by 1.30 p.m. Just half an hour into the course introductions we realised that the group would take a break whenever they felt like it rather than when we planned one in, and at best we could expect up to twenty of our twenty-six delegates to be with us at any one time. It was a bit of a free-for-all to be honest and something I certainly hadn't expected.

Once into the training we soon got used to accents and sayings that we didn't understand. We had a mostly lovely group and they did their best to make us feel welcomed. We had a few laughs along the way too. I remember on day three we were using a fairly basic personality test. It was a well-known one and some of the scenarios just didn't make sense to our group. Ideally the group complete the test individually, in silence, then we analyse it together and share our results. Bless Sharon, she had to read out each scenario and explain its meaning in basic language so the group could apply the best score that suited their personality and behaviour. For me it was like pulling teeth so I can only imagine how the group felt. We did laugh about that activity afterwards… especially when each individual revealed their predominant personality type.

Our 1.30 p.m. end of the day couldn't have come soon enough as the outdoor pool beckoned. It was forty-eight degrees in the sun so a relaxing dip and a meal in the air-conditioned American restaurant was a perfect end to a most interesting day. Overall our five days in Kuwait was a wonderful experience and left us with memories that we still chuckle about now.

Chapter nine

When Alcohol Gets in the Way

Don't worry; I haven't gone all saintly in this chapter. My racing friends would be the first to confirm that I do enjoy a gin or two when I'm out. Indeed, my eldest daughter would also confirm that I have been known to enjoy a 'gin in a tin' on a public bus on the way to the racecourse before now. She would also tell you about what happened when I dropped the half full tin on the floor of the bus and how the non-racegoing passengers reacted.

Occasionally alcohol has had an impact on the training course I'm delivering and an emergency rethink on my part has been necessary.

Take the course I was running in a hotel in the West Midlands. It just so happened that on the same day, the hotel was hosting a wedding down the corridor from my training room. In fact, the only thing separating my room and the wedding suite was a coffee area with free drinks and snacks available all day. It was early afternoon and we took our scheduled tea break before starting the next session on our agenda. I usually suggest a break of ten minutes, and with the coffee area next to our room that would be ample time. After fifteen minutes, one of my female delegates had not come back into the room, so I set the group a task to do on their own and went off for a wander looking for Julie. I didn't have to look far. She knew one of the guests at the wedding and was found in the wedding suite sat with a group of, rather loud and perhaps a little drunk, 'friends'.

I politely asked her to come back into the training room and Julie's only response was, "Can I bring my champagne with me?" With a sympathetic yet assertive response from me, she got up and walked behind me towards the door… without her glass of champagne in hand.

Now all present and correct in the training room we could pick up from where we were before the tea break, so I introduced the objectives for the final session of the day. Just two minutes later the door flung open and two of the wedding guests burst in and brought Julie an overflowing glass of champagne. My slightly less sympathetic and slightly more assertive tone ushered the two guests out of the room and I promptly locked the training room door so they couldn't make another alcohol delivery. All was okay again and we continued at pace to the end of the course. Julie's untouched glass of champagne stayed on the table throughout the rest of the afternoon. How I managed not to swig it down when the group weren't looking I will never know.

It would be unfair to only include a delegate experience in this chapter so I will try and balance things up by including an unfortunate incident that was caused by me in 2007. I've included the year as it's important that you don't think this was a recent event. I'd like to think that I learnt from it.

I was running a two-day course in London and one of the trainers who I knew well happened to be booked into the same hotel for the night in between.

We established this at lunch break on day one so she quickly made a plan for our evening ahead. Finish, the course at 4.30 p.m., head straight to the 'old fashioned boozer' round the corner till around eight p.m. then back to the hotel and order a pizza delivery. Sounded perfect and with a needy and tiring group this time, it was certainly something to look forward to at the end of the day.

The 'old fashioned boozer' was just as she'd described it. Sticky carpet, beer-stained mats, mahogany wood and a line of silver tankards above the bar. It certainly wasn't the swanky wine bar we could've chosen to visit in London that evening. Nevertheless, it served a good range of wines at a reasonable price, and this was a good thing as we managed to have quite a few. My colleague enjoyed a tipple most evenings, even when she was working, so I got the feeling she could have stayed drinking all night. I however was now feeling the effects at seven p.m. and suggested we bring forward our pizza phone call.

An hour later we were sat in her room with two boxes of deliciously smelling pizza on her bed. It's a bit like making a pancake… the first one is always tricky. The first slice of pizza was a challenge to get out of the box and needed some careful handling. After too much wine the word careful clearly didn't feature for me. I tugged at the cheesiest slice of loveliness and the whole thing ended up face down on her pristine, white cotton duvet cover. I laughed, she frowned and I ate it anyway. Why would I waste something that was going to soak up the wine and make things slightly more bearable in the morning?

Chapter ten

So sad…

Way back in 1991, in the days of ever-increasing regulation and standards, I found myself on an IIP working party. For those of you who are too young to know, IIP stands for Investors in People. As with most working parties for this particular organisation, it was a case of a Director getting a bunch of people together from across all main departments, briefing them on how important their role is, handing out a shed load of paper then setting an incredibly tight deadline before literally running out of the room before anyone could ask a question.

Sitting under the HR umbrella (even though I was a trainer not an HR professional), it seemed that a lot of the ground work in getting our organisation IIP accredited fell onto my shoulders. My working party colleagues seemed to think that it was their role to tell me how it wouldn't work in their department. With an already busy workload, and a team of trainers to line manage, I headed back to my desk with a head full of questions and disbelief. Before the end of the day though, there was a chink of something slightly better. I'd had an email telling me to attend an IIP global meeting the following week where all representatives from their respective businesses would be there. I felt hopeful in that they'd probably got a project plan and a way forward that I could tap into.

Fast forward a week and I'm sitting in a conference room with other IIP Champions; a title that had emerged the day before.

On my right was a very well-spoken lady who gave me the impression that this additional responsibility was very much beneath her and that she should never have been invited. In contrast, to my left was a chap, probably in his 20s, who was keen to find out as much as he could and go back to his office with a strategy to get things moving towards IIP accreditation as quickly as he could. Whilst it was a long day, it was productive and I did gain some confidence in the challenge ahead. The chap on my left mentioned that he had a meeting in my building the following Monday and could fit in an additional meeting with me to discuss the outputs from the day. This sounded like a great idea so a time and meeting place was agreed.

The following Monday arrived and he didn't show up. One hour moved to two hours of waiting for him, then I received a phone call. He'd been involved in a sporting activity over the weekend and had been killed. He was twenty-six. So sad.

Over the last thirteen years I have run possibly hundreds of courses on the subject of confidence, self-esteem and emotional resilience. The idea was to discuss and help delegates who brought their work-related experiences to the course, and in the main this is exactly what we discussed. For some however, their experiences went outside of the workplace and they recounted stories from home, from their childhood and occasionally from a personal relationship.

Whilst I have received training in counselling, I make it clear that I am not a qualified counsellor.

Certainly in the latter years of running these courses, I found that I was hearing more and more stories that shocked me to the core. Bullying in the workplace, violence in workplace toilets, coercion by manipulative and nasty line managers, even stalking by work colleagues that left people afraid to leave the building they operated from. One lady told me that she cancelled her holiday as she felt safest whilst at work and surrounded by her real colleagues. Most of the time, the delegates who were sharing these experiences were vocal, strong and relieved to be able to talk about them in a safe environment. Of course, I had to do the right thing and share some information with the senior management team if I feared that people were at risk, and sadly this is something I did fairly often.

Then there were the heartbroken, quiet and emotional delegates who had suffered a huge personal loss. The death of a baby or child, the loss of a home and a place to live, and probably the most frequently talked about loss, when a spouse or partner dies. These were the experiences I struggled with most. I've had a whole room of delegates in tears before and whilst it confirms that these people appreciated a place to talk and share, I couldn't help feeling guilty when I received a 100% satisfaction score for the course and all I'd done is listen and suggest a few things to help them in the future. So sad.

But without doubt the saddest of all was my story. A day when I was over an hour away from home and I tell my group in the introduction that I will keep my phone out and on loud as my Dad was receiving 'end of life' care.

Sure enough, by lunchtime I had received a message to say that Dad was fading so I did the only thing I could, and end the course early with a promise to rebook it. After a fast and probably not so safe drive to Dad in his nursing home, I was grateful to be able to spend his last hour holding his hand before he drifted away. Yes I felt guilty for leaving a room of delegates after only a few hours with them, but I'd have regretted it for the rest of my life if I had stayed until the scheduled finish time.

What I hadn't considered was how I would feel the next time I was delivering in the same venue. Let's just say that it was the hardest training day of my life and how I got through till the end of the day I will never know. What made it worse was that I was in exactly the same training room as I was on that previous occasion. So sad.

Chapter eleven

Lost for Words

I used to really enjoy the opportunity to facilitate a team activity with a group of emotionally intelligent professionals. It was so interesting to watch individual personality traits and behaviours emerge, and see how people react to common workplace challenges such as disagreements, friction, competition and tight deadlines. Nine times out of ten the activities worked well and the feedback that I was able to share afterwards was received positively.

Having spent the morning taking a group of twelve scientists through a personality and behaviour-based questionnaire, I was now looking forward to introducing the afternoon activity: Cave Rescue. It's a fairly simple task where the group need to discuss, debate, rank and agree the order in which their fictional volunteers should be rescued from a cave. There was little preparation needed on my part so I was able to enjoy the amazing buffet supplied by the client.

I introduced the activity and explained what the group needed to do. As with most team activities, there's an element of contention built in so that some important skills like negotiation, listening, compromise and questioning can be displayed throughout. The paper information I handed out to the group supported what I'd already shared with them and added a further few layers of detail to consider.

And consider it they did… for all of two minutes. There was a ripple of whispering on one side of the table and a very vocal individual at the end who said something like "Lesley, we are not doing this. We refuse to get involved in such a ridiculous and pointless activity." I'd certainly experienced some reticence by groups in the past however never a group who flatly refused. With my polite and professional head firmly attached I explained the benefits of working through the activity and how it would build on the knowledge they had already gained about themselves and each other in the morning session. My explanation and reassurance did nothing but push them further away and then the unheard of happened.

One of the 'whisperers' on the table got out of their chair, walked to the buffet table and picked up a large bowl still half full with crisps. They held the bowl over the table in front of me and tipped the crisps over the activity handouts I was yet to pass round. Nobody laughed, and most of the group packed their belongings up and left the room. One individual stayed behind to help me clear up (those salt and vinegar crisps were particularly smelly and greasy), and said that the group were the worst team they'd ever had to work with. They apologised for what had happened and escorted me back to reception. I was home by 2.30 p.m.

As a trainer I like to think that I can respond to most things in a positive way, however I was and still am lost for words.

I've mentioned previously my involvement in running courses around self-esteem and confidence.

In a small, cosy training room in the City of London, I was running a confidence building course for four delegates. It was a public event which means that the delegates were from different organisations and therefore the chances of them knowing each other were pretty slim. On a course like this I believe that's a good thing as they're more likely to open up to each other about why they have low confidence.

One of the first activities is to get the delegates to consider something they're proud of. It can be anything from getting the job they went for, reaching a personal fitness milestone, helping a neighbour or friend or even trying out a new recipe. On the flipchart I'd written up two questions that I would ask each of the delegates once they'd shared the thing they were proud of.

- "What did you do to contribute to this proud achievement?"
- "How did it make you feel?"

I remember that one of the delegates responses was a particular qualification that meant he could now apply for promotion. He shared that he'd delayed the exam date so he had more time to revise and that he'd used a new technique for remembering all the key information. He was proud and relieved that he'd now passed.

John was the last out of the four to say anything and even after listening to his three colleagues he still couldn't think of anything he was proud of. He was a quiet chap who avoided eye contact most of the time and had looked pretty uncomfortable since walking into the training room an hour earlier. I suggested he keep thinking about it and perhaps by coffee break he would have remembered a proud moment to share.

Just a few minutes into the next part of the day, which was largely theory based, John sat upright, looked straight at me and told us that he'd thought of something. Phew, what a relief. I'd hate to think of him getting through the day and still not be able to come up with anything he was proud of.

With a tone of voice that we hadn't heard so far in the day, John told us that he had got his wife pregnant and they had recently had a little boy. I was stood up at the front of the room as John shared this and as I stood away and looked back at my flipchart questions I realised that the next part would be even more uncomfortable for him. The other three had now worked out that he was expected to tell us what he did to contribute and how it made him feel.

The group burst out laughing (even John), I was lost for words and, indeed, the only words that came out of my mouth were something like, "Let's celebrate John's proud moment by taking an early coffee break!"

It's true to say that after coffee break and for the rest of the day John was a different person.

Even though it was lonely at times, when staying in a hotel I would always keep myself to myself. Where possible I would eat in my room and even if there were delegates staying too I would choose not to socialise with them. My excuse was always to catch up on emails and work.

In a well-known budget type hotel, breakfast had to be taken in their restaurant. The familiar purple seating was as well-known to me as the buffet style cooked breakfast menu. You just had to declare your room number to the waitress with the A4 list of rooms and names, and the highlighter pen and you were shown to your table. One morning in Nottingham it was particularly busy and I had to queue to 'check-in' for breakfast. When asked I gave my room number and the waitress looked down the list to check that I'd already paid. If she'd have been a bit quicker with this numerical list, I doubt that the following would have happened. The chap behind me in the queue said something like, "Oh, I wish I'd have known you were in the next room; I'd have suggested we spend some time together." I probably gave him a horrified look and was quickly ushered away by the slow reading waitress. Thankfully she then placed him on the furthest table away from me only a moment later. Breakfast was eaten and after checking out of the hotel I made my way to the training venue.

I was expecting a group of twelve delegates and sure enough they all arrived in good time. I always made an effort to greet them individually as this counts as a very important first impression. Sadly for one delegate it was my second impression.

The chap who'd made the inappropriate comment about being in the next hotel room to me had just walked into my training room. Initially lost for words, I straightened my professional and polite head, walked up to him, shook his hand and welcomed him to the course. I'm sure my piercing eye contact and very firm handshake didn't go unnoticed, and let's just say that during the first coffee break he'd apologised to me twice. What an idiot!

Chapter twelve

If I had a Pound…

This chapter needs little introduction. Over the years you start to realise that some of the phrases you hear from delegates are fairly predictable. I know that when I used to share some of them with my trainer friends, they had heard them too. You not only hear what a delegate is saying out loud, you have a good idea of what they're also thinking.

Here are some of the most common phrases I heard.

What they say	What they're thinking and don't want you to know
I've attended a similar course so will probably not contribute much on this one	I haven't got a clue and don't want to be here
You're the best trainer I've ever had	If my manager asks anything about me, please say nice things
There's nothing wrong with my leadership skills; it's my team who have the attitude	A recent staff survey has highlighted what my team really think of me
I need to leave early to get	There are some good shops

my train	on the way back to the station

What they say	**What they're thinking and don't want you to know**
I'm on this course to use up what's left in the training budget. I don't really need it	My manager has told me I need it and I disagree
My handwriting is awful so can somebody else scribe (write on the flipchart)	I can't be bothered to get out of my seat

Believe me, there are probably over hundred 'stock phrases' that I would hear often. They always used to make me smile… discreetly of course!

In my latter years I ran a significant number of courses in hospitals and would always carry my trainer's equipment; flipchart pens, white tac, laptop and cable, delegate materials etc in a laptop bag. If I had a pound for every time I was stopped by a member of the public and asked a medical question. They must've mistaken me for a doctor as I've been asked questions about waiting lists, and once even wound dressings. I do remember one elderly lady in a lift asked me If I'd just finished a long shift. She must've thought I looked really tired too!

The preventative measure was easy, however. I swapped my laptop bag for a High Street canvas bag and, hey presto, I was never mistaken for a doctor again.

If I had a pound… I'd be a millionaire Rodney.

Chapter thirteen

A Painful Day

One Spring, chilly day I was heading to London to deliver a course. I'd been looking forward to this one for ages as the venue was opposite Harrods, and whilst I'd not been there before, I'd been told that the training room had a balcony that overlooked the front entrances to the store. Perfect for some people watching and even a spot of shopping, should time allow.

My train arrived into Paddington at its usual time, and by 8.20 a.m. I was walking past the V&A museum, thinking how fortunate I was to have these opportunities in my work life. It was at that moment that my fortunate thoughts dried up as my foot had landed awkwardly and I felt a sharp pain through my ankle. You may well be thinking that I was foolish for wearing heels but I wasn't; I was wearing some smart, leather, flat loafers. I felt faint and nauseous and stood against the wall of the museum to recover. I know I didn't have much further to walk so through gritted teeth and dreadful pain I made my way to the training venue.

If I'm feeling off colour, I never like to tell my delegates, as I wonder if that leads them to think that they'll get a less than great experience. Thankfully the training room was fairly small and with only six delegates attending I could sit around the table with them and not look out of place. As the morning progressed I could feel my foot swelling and the pain increasing. I definitely wasn't up for a lunchtime visit to Harrods. Typical!

Grateful for an out-of-date cereal bar in my bag that I now called lunch, I managed to survive the afternoon and finish slightly earlier than expected. I had already decided to hail a cab back to the train station, so just had to pack up and tidy the room then head for home. Easier said than done though as my foot was now so swollen it was almost bursting out of my shoe. With my emergency scissors (always with me to cut through the heavily taped boxes of delegate materials), I cut down both sides of my loafer in an attempt to free my elephant sized foot. Earlier I described my loafers as smart, leather and flat. They were also fairly pricey at just under £200 and this was only the second time I'd worn them. Typical!

Of course, by cutting my shoe I'd also made it very sloppy; a bit like a mule style shoe. I struggled to keep it on as I walked into Paddington station so made a swift journey into Accessorize and bought a pair of bright pink flip flops. I must have looked a real sight. A black trouser suit, some sparkly and very pink flip flops and a now purple ankle and foot.

In my haste to board the train I'd forgotten to buy a sandwich for the journey. Apart from the cereal bar I called lunch I'd eaten nothing all day. Let's just say that the strong painkillers I took as we pulled out of London had a strange effect on me and I remember nothing about the train journey home. I hope I didn't snore.

Chapter fourteen

Interesting Training Rooms

Back in the '80s and early '90s, a training room was exactly that. A rectangular room with a trainer's desk at the front and a U-shape arrangement for the delegates to sit at; ensuring everyone had a good view of the trainer, each other and of course the flipchart pad and screen. The bulky overhead projector had to go just where you wanted to stand at the front, and it was a constant effort to remember the plug lead trailing across the floor and into the wall behind you. If you were lucky there would be a refreshments table at the back of the room with water, coffee and tea and a kettle. If you were even luckier you would have a representative from the onsite canteen turn up regularly in their net hat to replenish the table with hot water and fresh milk. VIP guests would also get the five-star treatment with a plate of biscuits; this happened to me only a few times. Jammy Dodgers in the middle, pink wafers and chocolate digestives around the edge and a few Morning Coffee biscuits that were often the last to be eaten up. It would always make me cross that the 'tea refresher' would walk into your room without knocking, wheeling a very squeaky trolley in front of them and proceed to remove the dirty china cups and saucers whilst making as much noise as they could.

Thankfully, businesses started to evolve and looked to offer a more conducive approach to learning. Hard chairs were replaced with brightly coloured felt sofas and break-out areas were popular for impromptu meetings and huddles.

And because we all get thirsty at different times of the day, coffee machines started to appear and were of course, available to use at any time. In the poshest of offices, shiny bean to cup coffee machines would sit in pride of place and be surrounded by little packets of shortbread, chocolate chip cookies and honey and ginger biscuits. As I've mentioned before, OHP machines were replaced with laptops and even the setup of the training room started to look more like a wedding reception with small tables and trendy reclining chairs. Branded pens, notepads and name cards were also something to expect and certainly a step up from a plain pencil and A5 pad.

What I've just described was fairly typical for the majority of my course deliveries, however occasionally I was surprised by the room offered to me. I guess you could say that a professional and accomplished trainer should be able to deliver a course anywhere, yet some of these environments pushed even the very best to their limits.

<u>A screen off</u> – The lecture theatre in a large teaching hospital had been double booked so a corner of it was screened off and both planned events were to go ahead at the same time. The large area of the theatre was an exhibition and display of some new clinical procedure, and my corner was where I would be based to deliver a half-day session on emotional resilience.

The screens were made of fabric and on wheels and whilst my handful of delegates sat in our cosy corner, considering how they can improve their levels of resilience, elbows, arms and goodness knows what else would poke through the screens from the exhibition side. It was noisy and so unproductive. Thankfully it was only a half-day event and I did manage to learn a little about a new style of catheter. Those exhibitions can be so interesting.

<u>Smoky bacon or ready salted?</u> – Now you would think that delivering a course in a food factory would have its benefits. Free samples maybe and mouth-watering posters adorning the walls of the training room. Both were true, however a long day in a crisp factory was beginning to take its toll. The room I had been allocated was where the flavour tasting happened. There was a long board room table and I was told that each place would have a few small bowls of crisps for the tasting team to sample and vote on. Of course today that wasn't happening, yet the smell in the training room was unreal. A slight tweak in the recipe of any crisp flavour would need to be tested, discussed and voted on before the change was made real. The day before the smoky bacon crisp recipe had been up for renewal. I honestly can't describe what I could smell, yet words like pig farm and pork scratchings may have featured in my description had I have tried. Every surface in that room was covered with boxes of crisps. Ready salted to my right, and next to that the prawn cocktail. On my left were the cheese and onion and cheese and salad cream. The boxes were open and we were free to eat as many packets as we wanted, as long as

we didn't leave the factory with so much as a single crisp.

When it comes to food, restraint rarely features for me; especially if we're talking savoury and snacky, yet because the delegates work with crisps day in day out they didn't touch a packet. Not one single crisp passed their lips. I've been told that this is the case of the workers in the chocolate factory too. Whilst they are allowed to eat as much chocolate at work as they would like, they rarely eat any. I can't fathom that one out at all.

So, I don't know what was worse that day. The strong smell that lingered from the previous days taste testing, the ongoing temptation whilst surrounded by more boxes of crisps than a Booker warehouse or the fact that I couldn't take a packet out of the building to enjoy on my drive home.

<u>In the wake of</u> – Occasionally maintenance issues mean that courses have to be cancelled at very short notice, or even on the day itself. I was running a one-day course and at lunch break was told that there was a plumbing problem that meant the whole training centre had to shut for emergency repairs. Rather than cancel the afternoon session, my course was transferred to a nearby clubhouse. We would be able to carry on the course in their bar area where complimentary refreshments would be available. It was only a five-minute drive away and with a group of excited delegates we pitched up in our new venue for the afternoon.

I had a lively group and we'd had a good morning together, and the free drinks only added to their enthusiasm. We were probably quite loud and it was a course where lots of ideas could be thrown around the room for discussion and debate.

Around an hour into the session, the clubhouse manager came into the bar and asked if we would contain the enthusiasm and volume and be a little more respectful. I must have looked surprised or like I hadn't understood what he'd said, as he got up close to me and whispered something like, "I shouldn't have to remind you that there is a wake happening in the next room." Of course I did the obvious thing which was to apologise and then explain that I didn't know that a wake was going on at the same time as our course. He simply nodded and walked out of the bar.

I shared this new knowledge with my group and we decided to take a quick break before continuing for the last part of the day. This was also a good opportunity to apologise to anyone who looked like they were attending the wake; the last thing I wanted to do was to offend anyone on such a sad occasion.

I needn't have worried. I walked past the open door of the wake and saw something that could have easily been viewed as a boozy, happy celebration party. I even saw a couple of mature ladies dancing on a table! I'm not sure what that Clubhouse Manager saw when he checked in on the wake gathering, however I only hope that when I depart this life, my friends and family have as good a knees-up as that one.

In case you're wondering, for those of you who know me well, I did finish the rest of the course in a more sedate manner – as requested. And no, I didn't join the two ladies dancing on the table.

<u>A day in the triffids</u> – This was another case of a double booking, however rather than be screened off like in the

hospital, my course was moved to a completely different area of the hotel. My room for the day was stunning. It was an orangery with a spectacular view of the impressive hotel gardens and hills in the distance. I had a fairly large group and it took me a while to lay out all the course materials, pads, pens and the usual paraphernalia. Before I knew it the first delegates were starting to make themselves comfortable. Just like I had, they entered the room with eyes wide open and a "wow" as they took in their surroundings for the day.

As the seats started to fill however we realised that there were a few green obstacles that would hinder our experience. The palm trees, the ivy and just about every other orangery plant imaginable were now literally in the faces of the group. Turn one way to avoid the trailing plant from the ceiling and you'd be poked in the eye by a sharp leaf or knocked on the head by a six-foot-tall plant pot. As beautiful as it was, the room was totally impractical to run a training session in with anything more than four people.

So, within thirty minutes, we'd opened the French doors onto the patio and moved their chairs into the sun. For the first time in my life I was running a course in the outdoors. What a perfect day that was, and no matter how beautiful and well equipped a training room was after that day, nothing would beat our garden experience.

<u>Please nurse, I need the toilet</u> – As in most healthcare buildings, space is at a premium. Course dates are almost always scheduled around the availability of the room, and in some cases this meant compromising. Perhaps a large group of twelve delegates would have to be split into two

groups of six and trained on different days as the room just wasn't large enough. Or you would be scheduled to deliver a full day event and have to pack up your room after the morning session and move the materials and delegates into a different room to continue in the afternoon.

In one particular hospital, my training room was not only surrounded by patient filled wards, it was half of an existing ward. It still had the rails on the ceiling for the curtains to hang around each bed, and a sink on each wall for constant hand washing and goodness knows what else. The red emergency call buttons were still wired into the walls and now covered over with yellow tape and a large sign saying 'Do not press'. None of these features in the training room were a real problem, unless the room was really full and you were the one delegate with your back up against the ceramic sink. Even then I used to move the tables around to ensure everyone was as comfortable as they could be, even if they couldn't see much around them. There was one feature that I couldn't control however, and that was the noise coming from behind the paper-thin partition wall. Behind it was the other half of the ward and it was almost always filled with patients. The hospital didn't offer major surgery and therefore took in patients who needed some rehabilitation and recuperation. What I'm saying is that they sounded quite mature in age, a little confused at times and definitely very vocal throughout the day.

Breakfast time for the ward seemed to last for hours. Whilst setting up my room before the delegates arrived, I would hear the nursing staff offering cereals, toast, tea and coffee. An hour into my course, so about 9.30 a.m., and I would still hear patients asking for more toast or complaining that they'd spilt their tea over them and their bed. All my delegates worked in the healthcare industry and really didn't seem phased about the vocal interruptions coming from the other side of the wall.

There were a few instances that brought course progress to a halt though, and we just had to laugh… discreetly.

"Nurse, I need a poo."

"Nurse I've done a poo."

"Nurse I'm wetting the bed when I cough."

"Nurse, she over there is staring at me."

"Nurse, he's taken all his clothes off and I don't like it."

And then you'd get the patients who used a swear word in almost every sentence. The nursing staff would tell them off, the patient would do it even more, and before you knew it you'd have a Healthcare Assistant knocking on your training room door to apologise for what they knew we had all heard.

None of this was a problem. We would have a chuckle, sometimes a joke where we would give a certain voice a name, and we would carry on with the course. I actually missed these days after the training was moved into a large, corporate, soundproofed lecture theatre. I wondered if 'Mabel' and 'Vincent' were still in that ward.

Chapter fifteen

Escape from the Floods

The local newspapers were flooded with this news, local and national news bulletins on tv were flooded with this news, and my home county was flooded… literally. On July 20th 2007 a deluge of 78mm of rain fell in just twelve hours. And to make things even worse, the local Water Treatment works that fed clean water to over 5,000 homes and businesses was also flooded. It was labelled as the county's biggest ever peacetime emergency.

Ok, so my home wasn't directly affected by the flooding and I could still drive down a few roads and get to the supermarket for supplies. By the end of that day however, the taps ran dry. Initially told that we would be without water for twenty-four hours soon extended to forty-eight hours, and by the weekend two litre bottles of drinking water were being dropped by the council on street corners and in car parks for locals to collect free of charge.

The following week I was due to deliver a two-day course in York. I had my hotel booked and was planning to drive rather than take the train. After five days of having no tap water and using stored rain water in our bathrooms and bottled water to drink and cook I decided that we had to take the opportunity of heading to York as a family. Thankfully I was able to change my hotel booking to a family room to accommodate the four of us, and off we went, escaping the water, media attention and stress of home.

I've often thought that being a trainer is a lonely job; especially if you have to stay away from home. It was so lovely to incorporate a work trip with my family and explore a city we'd previously visited many years ago. We went out for dinner, we explored the city on foot, and I was even dropped off and picked up from my training venue. Something I could certainly get used to. After two days of training we packed the car up with as many bottles of water we could manage and headed for home. It was a good job we did as the taps were still dry when we got back and running water didn't reappear for another nine days.

So, the moral of the story is, wherever possible, incorporate your trips away from home with friends, family and anyone else you enjoy being with. Like I said, it's a lonely life sometimes.

Chapter sixteen

Roleplay Roulette

Yep I know, it's a strange title for a chapter.

Verb: Roleplay.

'Act out or perform the part of a person or character, for example as a technique in training or psychotherapy.'

Noun: Roulette.

'A gambling game in which a ball is dropped on to a revolving wheel with numbered compartments, the players betting on the number at which the ball comes to rest.'

Roleplay activities are used often in face-to-face training, to encourage the delegates to play the role of a position they've been learning about in the course. Common examples are a recruiter or an appraiser. Maybe the delegates haven't conducted an interview before and need to not only understand the process and structure, but also demonstrate the skills required to do a good job. Line managers who are receiving training on how to conduct a formal disciplinary meeting will often do a roleplay and get some feedback from the trainer on where they need to improve before they hold a real meeting back in the workplace.

My use of the word roulette is simple. On the roulette wheel you can't predict where the ball will land. Will it be a single or double number? Will it be a red or a black compartment?

Conducting a roleplay session is pretty similar as you really can't predict how it will go. Will the 'recruiter' be a stern-faced interviewer who keeps the person being interviewed on the edge of their seat by asking tough, unemotional questions? At worst even, make them cry. Or does the interviewer feel so uncomfortable with this whole roleplay thing that they fall into fits of giggles every time the other person speaks. It's fair to say that I've seen a good range of both and a whole lot in between.

The cheesy one

Roleplay scenario	What was said/done
A recruitment interview	Last question at the end of the interview was "If you were a sandwich, what would you be and why?"

The funny one

Roleplay scenario	What was said/done
Disciplinary and grievance meeting	All the key points had been discussed and right at the end the 'manager' said "Just one final point, you also have BO. Have you heard of using deodorant?"

The one where I had to step in

Roleplay scenario	What was said/done
Annual appraisal meeting	The 'manager' accused the team member of being racist.

It never surprised me how many delegates said after the activity that they were roleplaying a behaviour that they had experienced for themselves. Either a line manager who had no clue about how to conduct an appraisal, or an interviewer who was totally inappropriate with their range of questions. Thank goodness for these types of courses.

Thankfully some companies insist that their staff cannot be a live interviewer until they have completed this course and been signed off by the trainer as competent. I certainly wish that had been the case when I experienced some interesting questions and behaviours back in the day. I wonder how the one question I remember from an interview in 1981 would stack up today…

"Lesley, you've said on your application form that you enjoy going to discos. How often do you do this and on what nights of the week?"

Chapter seventeen

Free guided tours

My journey to a training venue that I'd not visited before was usually dominated by two key emotions:

Excitement – what will the room be like, what will the facilities be like, what will the culture and feel of the organisation be like?

Trepidation – will I find it, will I like it, will I like them?

No matter what it and they were like however, a group of delegates who were really looking forward to the course and were proud to work for their organisation, was the best combination of all. I honestly think that I could have delivered a course in a stationery cupboard if the group really wanted to be there.

On many training days I would be lucky to see anything more than the reception area, the inside of a lift and my training room. Who knows what would have happened if the fire alarm had sounded and I'd have been on my own. I rarely received the health and safety briefing from a host that I should have had and was often given only very briefest of instructions on how to find my training room. I have however, been extremely fortunate to have had some personalised guided tours over the years. Delegates have been eager to give up their lunch break or time after the course, to show me the inner workings of their workplaces; and I've been truly amazed.

Here's my carefully considered, top five experiences of when this happened:

1	In Basel, Switzerland, I had a tour of a seed and crop generation plant. I was mostly fascinated by the efforts and engineering that went into ensuring all seeds received the correct amount of hydration and climate to grow. It reminded me of being in Universal Studios in Florida too as my mode of transport around the plant was a mini train. I listened to some classical music whilst being driven round and told about each of the plant areas. What a lovely hour that was.
2	This one happened in a food packaging factory in Shropshire. I was running a modular programme which meant that I saw the same group for six days; spread out over three months. The group said that they'd arranged a tour of the factory for me on the last day which I was looking forward to. What they hadn't told me about was the mesh hairnet I'd have to wear in two of the rooms. It was a blue, nylon net which came in one size only; small! For those who know me and my curls, just think medusa. Honestly I looked ridiculous with these spring curls poking through the holes in the net. As fascinating as it was to see how the food was bagged up in portion sizes for prisoners, I desperately needed to get that hairnet off.

3	I've delivered many courses in some very secure venues, some where I couldn't have possibly imagined what they'd be like on the inside. A particular set of dates loomed in my diary and I have to admit, they weren't dates that I was looking forward to. The course I was due to deliver was familiar and something I'd personally written, however the venue was a first for me. It was a nuclear power station surrounded by media attention and controversy and I'd even been told that a witch camped outside the gate. I had such a nice group that I didn't have the heart to say no to a tour, and by the end of the course I was a little bit curious. I won't share too much about it, other than to say, it was very loud, very large and the metal bridge I was standing on to get the best view of the nuclear reactor had more holes than metal so I could see everything below me. Scary, scary, scary and I couldn't wait to get into the safety and quiet of my own car to drive home. I even smiled at the tent pitched on the grass outside the main gate. I wonder if the witch was in residence that day?
4	When I visited Dubai in 2006 to deliver a course, I had some time to explore. The lovely driver/chauffeur that my hotel sourced for me knew the Sheikh who was overseeing the new build Atlantis Palm Hotel so he took me to see the early stages of development. The Sheikh's office was gold, marble, opulent and opposite the seven-star hotel The Burj Al Arab. I was so impressed by the breathtaking view that I made an immediate pact

	with myself. One day I would dine in The Burj Al Arab. The Atlantis Palm was very much still in the building phase however the scaled model of what it would become was incredible. I was offered strong Arabic coffee and petit fours and the Sheikh took great delight in telling me about his other buildings in Dubai. I left feeling that I had been treated like a queen and vowed to return one day. Nine years later my pact came true and I got to dine on the twenty-fourth floor of The Burj Al Arab. The Atlantis Palm was fully on view and glistening in the Arabian sun. How lucky was I?
5	I'm not a sporty kind of girl, however I do enjoy tennis and horse racing; as a spectator. An opportunity to deliver a training course in Headingley Cricket Ground was treated in the same way as most of my previous training venues. Ok, so it's in Leeds. Should I drive or take the train? Will I need to take a meal or will I be able to get something there? Can I park? I remember a male training colleague at the time saying that he would love to swap one of his events for this one as he loved cricket. Surely there wouldn't be a match playing whilst I was there? I couldn't understand what the fuss was all about. Well, I was right about one thing. There were no matches playing whilst I was there, however the venue itself was a truly unique training experience. My 'hotel room' for the night overlooked the ground, and my training room to deliver the course was absolutely fascinating. Cricket paraphernalia everywhere and a tour had been

planned for me and my group of delegates. We got to see the museum part of the ground where some apparently famous cricketers had played back in the day and their bats and other artifacts were proudly displayed. I still don’t understand cricket, mind you.

There were a few more tours I could have mentioned; police headquarters including cells, medical laboratory and a supported housing establishment for vulnerable people.

I do need to briefly mention the one tour I gracefully declined though; a morgue in a large city hospital. I’m not sure how I would have responded to that one, however I do know that there are some very interesting and caring people who manage them in the UK. All credit to them as I know it’s something I couldn’t do.

Chapter eighteen

Smelly Pens

As an occasional delegate myself I loved to walk into a training room and see a bright and cheerful message on the flipchart, welcoming me to the course. Firstly, it confirmed that I was actually in the right room (you would be amazed at how many delegates have walked into my room only to realise that they should be somewhere else). Secondly, I believe that any visual creations in the training room are a 'moment of truth' or first impression and perhaps tell us something about the trainer or the style of the course itself.

For example, if I saw the word welcome written in a black flipchart marker and nothing else on that oversized piece of paper, I would automatically think that little effort had been made. Obviously I couldn't prove or disprove this until later, however I might also think basic and boring. Harsh words I know, yet to me, that moment of truth that is gauged when a delegate enters the room for the first time is key and not to be wasted.

You may be reading this and thinking that a pad of flipchart paper is so unnecessary when we live in a world of technology, and in this case, digital slides showing on a large screen on the wall. They of course are a visual creation therefore the same principal applies. Make that first slide as welcoming and cheerful as you can. It helps to set the tone for the whole event.

To those people who believe they are visual learners, i.e., they learn through their eyes and remember what they saw rather than what they heard, then colour is really important. In my early years of delivering training courses, a pack of flipchart markers would comprise just four colours. Black, green, red and blue, and they'd all have a fat, chunky bullet tip that made your writing look clumsy until you got used to them. Thankfully over time I discovered the best flipchart markers a trainer can own; Mr Sketch Scented Markers. Not only were there twelve different colours, they had a strong smell and were non-toxic.

How can anyone; trainer or delegate, resist using a bright pink raspberry scented pen that reminded you of the pink, shiny refresher sweets that you buy wrapped in green and yellow paper. They even smelt 'fizzy' in my opinion. The black one was a dark, inky black and smelt of liquorice, and was a bit like marmite. You either loved it or hated it. I loved it, although it became overpowering if you used it on every piece of flipchart paper in the room. The pale green one was minty and smelt like toothpaste, and the yellow one was too pale to use at a distance however great as a fresh, lemony highlighter. As you can probably tell, I loved my smelly pens and I assumed that all my delegates did too.

As an energizer after coffee or lunch break I would hand out the pens to small groups and ask them to guess the smell. I felt that it was a low-risk method of encouraging people to talk to each other, and believe me, it was sometimes needed. Much better than 'pulling teeth' with a quiet and disinterested group, which thankfully didn't happen to me that often.

So, the reason I'm sharing this with you still makes me chuckle when I think about it. I occasionally had an unpredictable response from delegates who had just smelt the pens. There's a few that I couldn't possibly mention and have to leave in the censored category, however most of the responses were just funny.

The dark green pen – meant to smell like green apple – smelt like ear wax

The orange pen – meant to smell like tangerine – smelt like nan's net curtains

The brown pen – meant to smell like cinnamon – smelt like a hot circuit board

The yellow pen – meant to smell like lemon – smelt like the toilets at work or a baby's wet nappy.

The orange description made me laugh the most. I don't remember ever smelling my nan's net curtains!

Had I have carried on working past March 2020, I would have needed to purchase a new set of Mr Sketch Scented Markers. I cannot believe my luck as Mr Sketch has only gone and updated the box of smells and colours. I've missed out on the opportunity to try out the new Buttery Popcorn, the Pineapple, and the Nacho Cheese pens! Or have I…? I wonder if my baby Grandson is old enough to get a set in his Christmas stocking? Anyway, who wants to have a flipchart pad smelling of Nacho Cheese?

Chapter nineteen

Familiar Faces

I guess this was inevitable, although certainly not something that I had even thought about when I became a trainer. I would probably get to see or even meet a few famous people. I use the word famous lightly as some of those I've seen are most definitely famous, and others are well known. Either way it was a privilege to be in their company.

My most enjoyable discussion was with Louise Minchin. When she's not presenting BBC Breakfast on weekdays, she's either hosting a corporate event or training for her next triathlon. In case you were wondering, I wasn't stood amongst a bunch of triathletes, I was involved in running a corporate event that she would host in the afternoon. I enjoyed a brief chat over lunch where she told me about her gorgeous two daughters who would be dragging her off to the hotel swimming pool later. What a lovely, down to earth and easy to talk to person she is. Oh, and when she gets a fit of the giggles, it really is contagious!

The following year, at the same event, Mary Nightingale was the host. Usually presenting the ITV news, she took a day out of her busy schedule to join us. Again, whilst slightly more serious than Louise, she was a gracious and most interesting person to talk to. Honestly, anyone would think that I got involved in that event just to meet the celebs!

Of course, London is a great place for people watching and Marylebone High Street never let me down. A bench in a church garden and a Waitrose sandwich was all I needed to relax and wait. Too many famous faces to mention, however the highlights for me were the late Barbara Windsor and Ronnie Corbett. I was astonished that they were so tiny in height and whenever I see a mustard yellow corduroy suit, I still think of Ronnie Corbett.

Travelling was another great way to sit back and watch the world, well the people really, go by. A rushing Ben Fogle in Paddington train station to a relaxed and very chatty Mike Brewer on a flight to Aberdeen. Mike presents Wheeler Dealers, the car show, and he was going up to see an old vehicle he wanted to buy and renovate for the show.

If you remember, I used the word privilege in the opening paragraph of this chapter, and here's why. Somewhere in the West I was extremely fortunate to be in the company of some very well-known people.

HRH Prince Charles, Prince of Wales

HRH Prince William, Duke of Cambridge

Vice Admiral Sir Timothy Laurence

If that wasn't a real reminder of how fortunate I was to experience this whilst 'just doing my job', I don't know what was.

Conclusion

So, there you have it; the most memorable times in my long career. I actually found it incredibly hard to select the ones I wanted to share as there were literally hundreds to choose from. I could have probably written a book as long as War and Peace if I wanted to include all of them! Interestingly though, the key messages would have remained the same, so it's these that I'll leave you with.

Be professional – you cannot change others' behaviour yet you can choose how to respond.

Be discreet – we don't need to share everything we hear, see and sense.

Be prepared – for the unexpected.

Be kind – because behind the face that comes across as grumpy or aloof there may be an unhappy or anxious individual who faces more challenges than we could ever imagine.

I hope you enjoyed reading Flipcharts and Faux Pas,

Lesley x